Travel Dreams

FUN-SCHOOLING

JOURNAL

*An Adventurous Approach
to Geography & Social Studies*

France

Spain

France

France

Greece

Greece

Greece

United Kingdom

TELEPHONE

Turkey

TRAVEL
DREAMS
FUN-SCHOOLING
JOURNAL

Name:

Date:

Contact Information:

About Me:

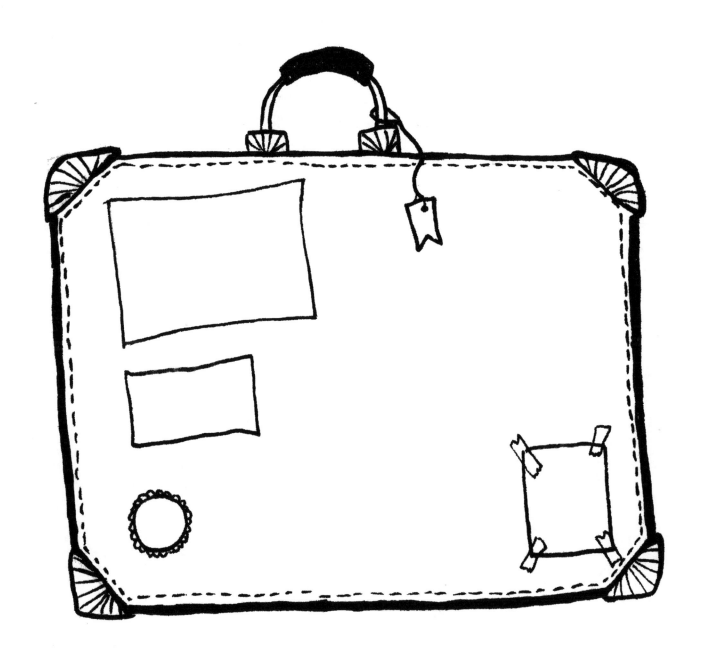

IF you could go anywhere in the WORLD, where would you go?

Travel Dreams Homeschool Journal
You are going to learn about 30 Interesting Places!

30 Fascinating Cities Around the World:

To Do List:

- Please be ready to visit your local library to pick out books.
- Zoom in to every location on Google Earth.
- Use online videos to learn about culture, food and history.

Go to the Library or Book Store to Pick Out:

- Four Travel Books (Look for Famous Cities & Natural Wonders)
- One Atlas or Book of Maps
- One Colorful Cookbook with Recipes from Around the World.

Books & Documentaries:

Pick out your books and ask your parents to help you choose documentaries that they approve of. You will need to watch 30 episodes.

Here are some options and ideas that can help you learn about travel, culture, communities and geographic curiosities all over the world:

- Ethnic Cooking
- Travel Documentaries
- Reality Travel Shows
- History of Interesting Places
- How People Live in Other Countries
- Travel Planning Tutorials
- Global Transportation

- Wildlife and Natural Wonders
- Cultural Traditions
- Natural Disasters
- Famous and Interesting People from around the World.
- Missionary Stories
- Where Scientific Discoveries Were Made

30 CITIES

Start by figuring out what continent each city is in:

CITY	COUNTRY	CONTINENT
Abu Dhabi	United Arab Emirates	
Amsterdam	Netherlands	
Budapest	Hungary	
Cape Town	South Africa	
Chicago	United States of America	
Hong Kong	China	
Istanbul	Turkey	
Jerusalem	Israel	
Las Vegas	United States of America	
London	England	
Lviv	Ukraine	
Montreal	Canada	
New York City	United States of America	
Panama City	Panama	

CITY	COUNTRY	CONTINENT
Paris	France	
Prague	Czech Republic	
Rio de Janeiro-	Brazil	
Rome	Italy	
Saint Petersburg	Russia	
San Francisco	United States of America	
Seattle	United States of America	
Shanghai	China	
Singapore	Singapore	
Stockholm	Sweden	
Sydney	Australia	
Tokyo	Japan	
Vancouver	Canada	
Venice	Italy	
Washington D.C.	United States of America	
Zurich	Switzerland	

Decorate These Suitcases When You Decide What Cities You Want to Visit in the Future:

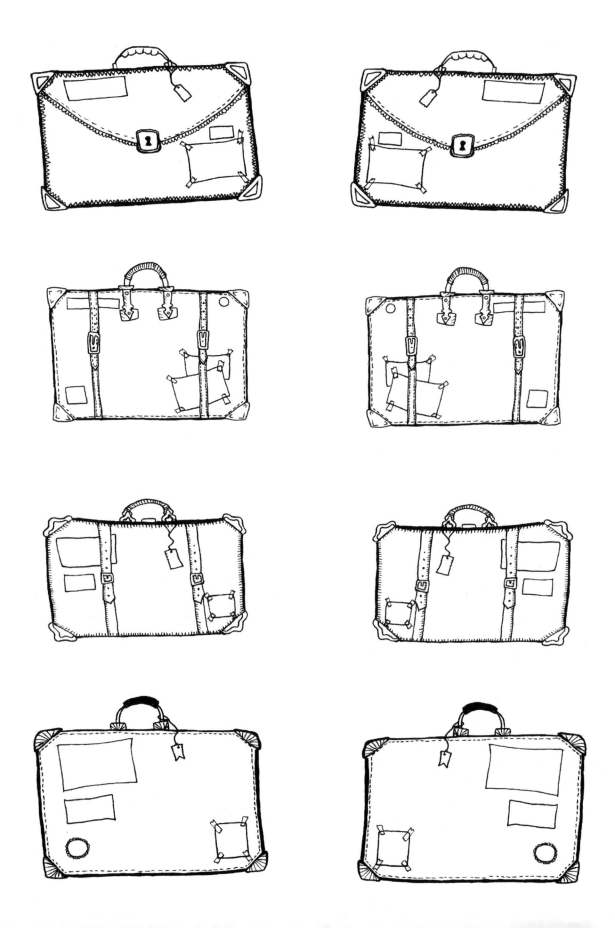

Choose Your Travel Books

1. Write down the titles and decorate each cover below.

2. Keep your stack of books in a safe place.

3. Be ready to read a few pages from your books daily.

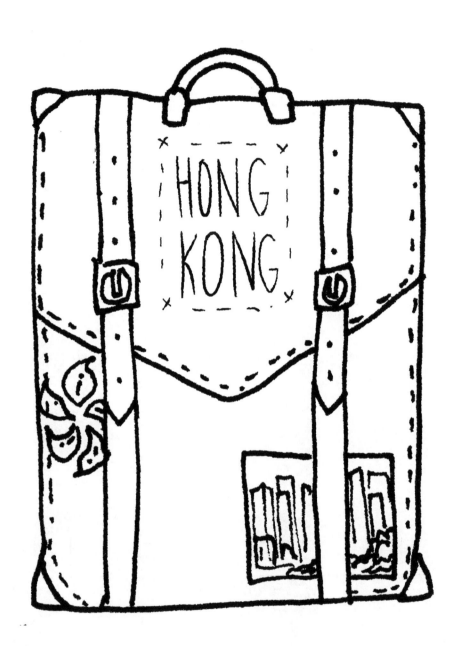

Where on earth are you going?

LABEL THE MAPS

WITH THE NAMES OF THE 30 CITIES

That You Are Learning About

Label Countries & Continents too!

PLot these
Cities oN the
World Map.

ROME

HONG KONG

SYDNEY

LONDON

NEW YORK

PARIS

TOKYO

TRAVEL MAP

Label the Continent, Color the Countries
and plot the Cities on this Map.
Use the List on Pages 6-7.

LIST OF PLACES

_____

_____

_____

_____

_____

_____

_____

_____

_____

_____

_____

_____

TRAVEL MAP

Label the Continent, Color the Countries and Plot the Cities on this Map. Use the List on Pages 6-7.

LIST OF PLACES

_____

_____

_____

_____

_____

_____

_____

_____

_____

_____

_____

_____

_____

TRAVEL MAP

Label the Continent, Color the Countries
and Plot the Cities on this Map.
Use the List on Pages 6-7.

LIST OF PLACES

_____

_____

_____

_____

_____

_____

_____

_____

_____

_____

_____

_____

TRAVEL MAP

Label the Continent, Color the Countries
and Plot the Cities on this Map.
Use the List on Pages 6-7.

LIST OF PLACES

_____

_____

_____

_____

_____

_____

_____

_____

_____

_____

_____

_____

_____

TRAVEL MAP

Label the Continent, Color the Countries
and Plot the Cities on this Map.
Use the List on Pages 6-7.

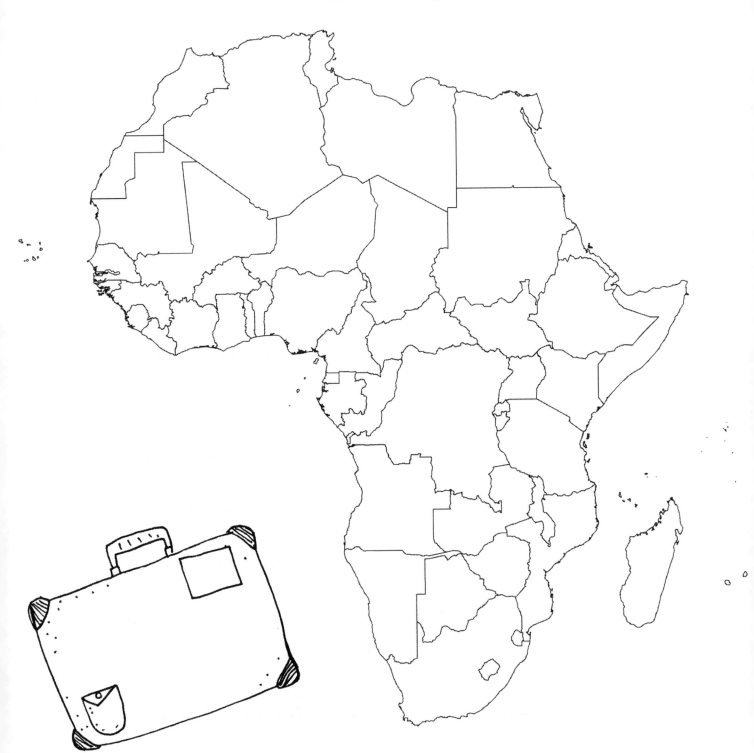

LIST OF PLACES

_____

_____

_____

_____

_____

_____

_____

_____

_____

_____

_____

_____

_____

TRAVEL MAP

Label the Continent, Color the Countries
and Plot the Cities on this Map.
Use the List on Pages 6-7.

LIST OF PLACES

_____

_____

_____

_____

_____

_____

_____

_____

_____

_____

_____

_____

My Travel Dreams

Abu Dhabi

ABU DHABI

UNITED ARAB EMIRATES

All About
ABU DHABI

Look in a Book
Look on Google Earth
Watch A Documentary

RESEARCH REFERENCES:

_____

_____

_____

NOTES:

_____

_____

_____

_____

_____

Write or Draw

Popular Foods:	Traditional Clothing:
Draw the Flag:	**A Quote or Proverb:**
A Historic Event:	**A Famous Landmark:**

Things to Know when Traveling to ABU DHABI

_____

_____

_____

_____

_____

_____

_____

_____

_____

_____

_____

What to See

Write about a Historic Event

ABU DHABI

_____

_____

_____

_____

_____

_____

_____

_____

_____

_____

_____

What to Do

Find a Recipe From
ABU DHABI

TITLE:

_____

Ingredients:

_____   _____

_____   _____

_____   _____

_____   _____

Instructions:

_____

_____

_____

_____

_____

Step by Step Food Prep:

1	2

3	4

5	6

All About Style

ABU DHABI

Fashion in the City

_____

_____

_____

_____

MODERN STYLES

Draw Traditional Costumes:

AMSTERDAM

AMSTERDAM

NETHERLANDS

All About
AMSTERDAM

Look in a Book
Look on Google Earth
Watch A Documentary

RESEARCH REFERENCES:

_____

_____

_____

NOTES:

_____

_____

_____

_____

Write or Draw

Popular Foods:	**Traditional Clothing:**
Draw the Flag:	**A Quote or Proverb:**
A Historic Event:	**A Famous Landmark:**

Things to Know
when Traveling to
AMSTERDAM

_____

_____

_____

_____

_____

_____

_____

_____

_____

_____

_____

What to See

Write about a Historic Event

AMSTERDAM

_____

_____

_____

_____

_____

_____

_____

_____

_____

_____

_____

_____

What to Do

Find a Recipe From
AMSTERDAM

TITLE:

_____

Ingredients:

_____   _____

_____   _____

_____   _____

_____

Instructions:

_____

_____

_____

_____

_____

Step by Step Food Prep:

1	2
3	4
5	6

All About Style

AMSTERDAM

Fashion in the City

_____

_____

_____

_____

MODERN STYLES

Draw Traditional Costumes:

BUDAPEST

HUNGARY

BUDAPEST

HUNGARY

Budapest, Hungary

All About

BUDAPEST

Look in a Book
Look on Google Earth
Watch A Documentary

RESEARCH REFERENCES:

_____

_____

_____

NOTES:

_____

_____

_____

_____

_____

Write or Draw

Popular Foods:	**Traditional Clothing:**
Draw the Flag:	**A Quote or Proverb:**
A Historic Event:	**A Famous Landmark:**

Things to Know when Traveling to
BUDAPEST

_____

_____

_____

_____

_____

_____

_____

_____

_____

_____

_____

_____

What to See

Write about a Historic Event
BUDAPEST

_____

_____

_____

_____

_____

_____

_____

_____

_____

_____

_____

_____

What to Do

Find a Recipe From
BUDAPEST

TITLE:

_____

Ingredients:

_____   _____

_____   _____

_____   _____

_____

Instructions:

_____

_____

_____

_____

Step by Step Food Prep:

1	2
3	4
5	6

All About Style

BUDAPEST

Fashion in the City

_____

_____

_____

_____

MODERN STYLES

Draw Traditional Costumes:

CAPE TOWN

SOUTH AFRICA

All About
CAPE TOWN

Look in a Book
Look on Google Earth
Watch A Documentary

RESEARCH REFERENCES:

_____

_____

_____

NOTES:

_____

_____

_____

_____

_____

Write or Draw

Popular Foods:	Traditional Clothing:
Draw the Flag:	A Quote or Proverb:
A Historic Event:	A Famous Landmark:

Things to Know
when Traveling to
CAPE TOWN

_____

_____

_____

_____

_____

_____

_____

_____

_____

_____

_____

What to See

Write about a Historic Event

CAPE TOWN

_____

_____

_____

_____

_____

_____

_____

_____

_____

_____

_____

_____

What to Do

Find a Recipe From

CAPE TOWN

TITLE:

_____

Ingredients:

_____   _____

_____   _____

_____   _____

_____

Instructions:

_____

_____

_____

_____

Step by Step Food Prep:

1	2
3	4
5	6

All About Style

CAPE TOWN

Fashion in the City

_____

_____

_____

_____

MODERN STYLES

Draw Traditional Costumes:

CHICAGO

UNITED STATES
OF AMERICA

All About
CHICAGO

Look in a Book
Look on Google Earth
Watch A Documentary

RESEARCH REFERENCES:

_____

_____

_____

NOTES:

_____

_____

_____

_____

_____

Write or Draw

Popular Foods:	Traditional Clothing:
Draw the Flag:	**A Quote or Proverb:**
A Historic Event:	**A Famous Landmark:**

Things to Know
when Traveling to
CHICAGO

_____

_____

_____

_____

_____

_____

_____

_____

_____

_____

_____

What to See

Write about a Historic Event
CHICAGO

_____

_____

_____

_____

_____

_____

_____

_____

_____

_____

_____

_____

What to Do

Find a Recipe From
CHICAGO

TITLE:

_____

Ingredients:

_____   _____

_____   _____

_____   _____

_____

Instructions:

_____

_____

_____

_____

_____

Step by Step Food Prep:

1	2
3	4
5	6

All About Style

CHICAGO

Fashion in the City

_____

_____

_____

_____

MODERN STYLES

Draw Traditional Costumes:

HONG KONG

CHINA

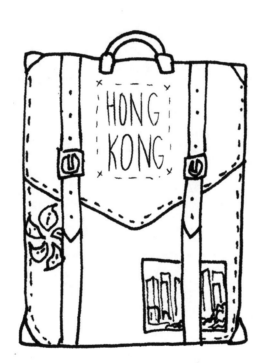

All About

HONG KONG

Look in a Book
Look on Google Earth
Watch A Documentary

RESEARCH REFERENCES:

_____

_____

_____

NOTES:

_____

_____

_____

_____

_____

Write or Draw

Popular Foods:	Traditional Clothing:
Draw the Flag:	A Quote or Proverb:
A Historic Event:	A Famous Landmark:

Things to Know
when Traveling to
HONG KONG

_____

_____

_____

_____

_____

_____

_____

_____

_____

_____

_____

What to See

Write about a Historic Event
HONG KONG

_____

_____

_____

_____

_____

_____

_____

_____

_____

_____

_____

_____

What to Do

Find a Recipe From
HONG KONG

TITLE:

_____

Ingredients:

_____   _____

_____   _____

_____   _____

_____

Instructions:

_____

_____

_____

_____

Step by Step Food Prep:

1	2
3	4
5	6

All About Style

HONG KONG

Fashion in the City

_____

_____

_____

_____

MODERN STYLES

Draw Traditional Costumes:

Islanbul Turkey

ISTANBUL

TURKEY

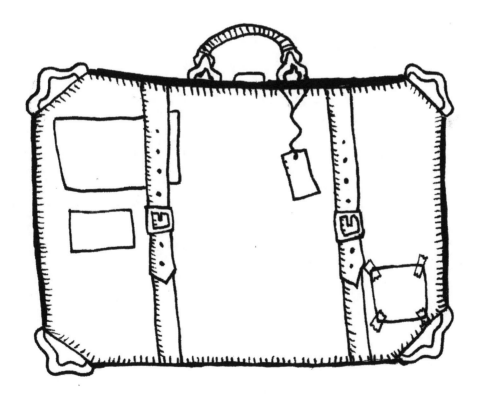

All About
ISTANBUL

Look in a Book
Look on Google Earth
Watch A Documentary

RESEARCH REFERENCES:

_____

_____

_____

NOTES:

_____

_____

_____

_____

Write or Draw

Popular Foods:	Traditional Clothing:
Draw the Flag:	**A Quote or Proverb:**
A Historic Event:	**A Famous Landmark:**

Things to Know when Traveling to ISTANBUL

_____

_____

_____

_____

_____

_____

_____

_____

_____

_____

_____

_____

What to See

Write about a Historic Event
ISTANBUL

_____

_____

_____

_____

_____

_____

_____

_____

_____

_____

_____

What to Do

Find a Recipe From
ISTANBUL

TITLE:

_____

Ingredients:

_____   _____

_____   _____

_____   _____

_____

Instructions:

_____

_____

_____

_____

_____

Step by Step Food Prep:

1	2
3	4
5	6

All About Style

ISTANBUL

Fashion in the City

_____

_____

_____

_____

MODERN STYLES

Draw Traditional Costumes:

Jerusalem

JERUSALEM

ISRAEL

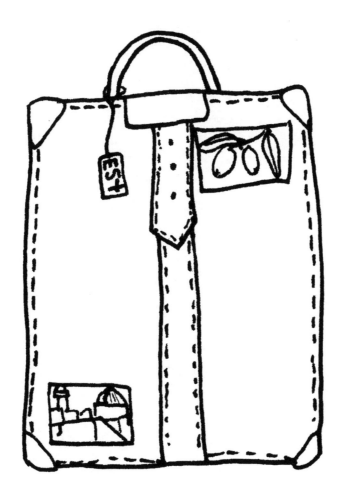

All About

JERUSALEM

Look in a Book
Look on Google Earth
Watch A Documentary

RESEARCH REFERENCES:

_____

_____

_____

NOTES:

_____

_____

_____

_____

_____

Write or Draw

Popular Foods:	Traditional Clothing:

Draw the Flag:	A Quote or Proverb:

A Historic Event:	A Famous Landmark:

Things to Know
when Traveling to
JERUSALEM

_____

_____

_____

_____

_____

_____

_____

_____

_____

_____

_____

_____

What to See

Write about a Historic Event

JERUSALEM

_____

_____

_____

_____

_____

_____

_____

_____

_____

_____

_____

_____

What to Do

Find a Recipe From
JERUSALEM

TITLE:

_____

Ingredients:

_____   _____

_____   _____

_____   _____

_____

Instructions:

_____

_____

_____

_____

Step by Step Food Prep:

1	2
3	4
5	6

All About Style

JERUSALEM

Fashion in the City

_____

_____

_____

_____

MODERN STYLES

Draw Traditional Costumes:

LAS VEGAS

UNITED STATES OF AMERICA

All About
LAS VEGAS

Look in a Book
Look on Google Earth
Watch A Documentary

RESEARCH REFERENCES:

_____

_____

_____

NOTES:

_____

_____

_____

_____

_____

Write or Draw

Popular Foods:	Traditional Clothing:

Draw the Flag:	A Quote or Proverb:

A Historic Event:	A Famous Landmark:

Things to Know when Traveling to LAS VEGAS

_____

_____

_____

_____

_____

_____

_____

_____

_____

_____

_____

What to See

Write about a Historic Event
LAS VEGAS

_____

_____

_____

_____

_____

_____

_____

_____

_____

_____

_____

_____

What to Do

Find a Recipe From
LAS VEGAS

TITLE:

_____

Ingredients:

_____ _____

_____ _____

_____ _____

_____

Instructions:

_____

_____

_____

_____

Step by Step Food Prep:

1	2
3	4
5	6

All About Style

LAS VEGAS

Fashion in the City

_____

_____

_____

_____

MODERN STYLES

Draw Traditional Costumes:

Big Ba

London

tea time

LONDON

ENGLAND

All About

LONDON

Look in a Book
Look on Google Earth
Watch A Documentary

RESEARCH REFERENCES:

_____

_____

_____

NOTES:

_____

_____

_____

_____

_____

Write or Draw

Popular Foods:	Traditional Clothing:
Draw the Flag:	**A Quote or Proverb:**
A Historic Event:	**A Famous Landmark:**

Things to Know
when Traveling to
LONDON

_____

_____

_____

_____

_____

_____

_____

_____

_____

_____

_____

What to See

Write about a Historic Event
LONDON

_____

_____

_____

_____

_____

_____

_____

_____

_____

_____

_____

_____

What to Do

Find a Recipe From
LONDON

TITLE:

_____

Ingredients:

_____   _____

_____   _____

_____   _____

_____

Instructions:

_____

_____

_____

_____

_____

Step by Step Food Prep:

1	2
3	4
5	6

All About Style

LONDON

Fashion in the City

MODERN STYLES

Draw Traditional Costumes:

LVIV

UKRAINE

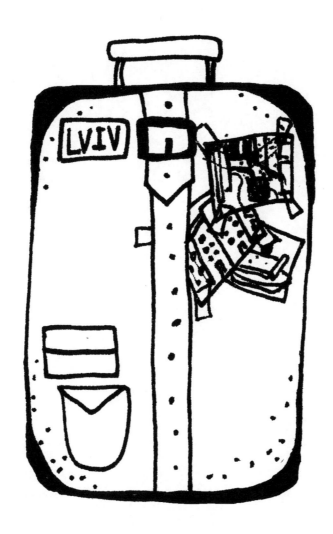

All About
LVIV

Look in a Book
Look on Google Earth
Watch A Documentary

RESEARCH REFERENCES:

_____

_____

_____

NOTES:

_____

_____

_____

_____

_____

Write or Draw

Popular Foods:	Traditional Clothing:

Draw the Flag:	A Quote or Proverb:

A Historic Event:	A Famous Landmark:

Things to Know
when Traveling to
LVIV

_____

_____

_____

_____

_____

_____

_____

_____

_____

_____

_____

What to See

Write about a Historic Event
LVIV

_____

_____

_____

_____

_____

_____

_____

_____

_____

_____

_____

_____

What to Do

Find a Recipe From
LVIV

TITLE:

_____

Ingredients:

_____ _____

_____ _____

_____ _____

_____

Instructions:

_____

_____

_____

_____

Step by Step Food Prep:

1	2
3	4
5	6

All About Style

LVIV

Fashion in the City

MODERN STYLES

Draw Traditional Costumes:

Montreal

MONTREAL

CANADA

All About
ABU DHABI

Look in a Book
Look on Google Earth
Watch A Documentary

RESEARCH REFERENCES:

_____

_____

_____

NOTES:

_____

_____

_____

_____

_____

Write or Draw

Popular Foods:	**Traditional Clothing:**
Draw the Flag:	**A Quote or Proverb:**
A Historic Event:	**A Famous Landmark:**

Things to Know
when Traveling to
MONTREAL

_____

_____

_____

_____

_____

_____

_____

_____

_____

_____

_____

What to See

Write about a Historic Event
MONTREAL

_____

_____

_____

_____

_____

_____

_____

_____

_____

_____

_____

_____

What to Do

Find a Recipe From

MONTREAL

TITLE:

_____

Ingredients:

_____ _____

_____ _____

_____ _____

_____

Instructions:

_____

_____

_____

_____

_____

Step by Step Food Prep:

1	2
3	4
5	6

All About Style

MONTREAL

Fashion in the City

_____

_____

_____

_____

MODERN STYLES

Draw Traditional Costumes:

NEW YORK CITY

USA

All About

NEW YORK CITY

Look in a Book
Look on Google Earth
Watch A Documentary

RESEARCH REFERENCES:

_____

_____

_____

NOTES:

_____

_____

_____

_____

_____

Write or Draw

Popular Foods:	Traditional Clothing:
Draw the Flag:	**A Quote or Proverb:**
A Historic Event:	**A Famous Landmark:**

Things to Know
when Traveling to
NEW YORK CITY

_____

_____

_____

_____

_____

_____

_____

_____

_____

_____

_____

What to See

Write about a Historic Event
NEW YORK CITY

_____

_____

_____

_____

_____

_____

_____

_____

_____

_____

_____

_____

What to Do

Find a Recipe From
NEW YORK CITY

TITLE:

_____

Ingredients:

_____   _____

_____   _____

_____   _____

_____

Instructions:

_____

_____

_____

_____

_____

Step by Step Food Prep:

1	2
3	4
5	6

All About Style

NEW YORK CITY

Fashion in the City

_____

_____

_____

_____

MODERN STYLES

Draw Traditional Costumes:

PANAMA CITY

PANAMA

All About

PANAMA CITY

Look in a Book
Look on Google Earth
Watch A Documentary

RESEARCH REFERENCES:

_____

_____

_____

NOTES:

_____

_____

_____

_____

_____

Write or Draw

Popular Foods:	Traditional Clothing:
Draw the Flag:	A Quote or Proverb:
A Historic Event:	A Famous Landmark:

Things to Know
when Traveling to
PANAMA CITY

_____

_____

_____

_____

_____

_____

_____

_____

_____

_____

_____

What to See

Write about a Historic Event
PANAMA CITY

_____

_____

_____

_____

_____

_____

_____

_____

_____

_____

_____

_____

What to Do

Find a Recipe From
PANAMA CITY

TITLE:

_____

Ingredients:

_____ _____

_____ _____

_____ _____

_____

Instructions:

_____

_____

_____

_____

Step by Step Food Prep:

1	2
3	4
5	6

All About Style

PANAMA CITY

Fashion in the City

_____

_____

_____

_____

MODERN STYLES

Draw Traditional Costumes:

PARIS

FRANCE

All About

PARIS

Look in a Book
Look on Google Earth
Watch A Documentary

RESEARCH REFERENCES:

_____

_____

_____

NOTES:

_____

_____

_____

_____

_____

Write or Draw

Popular Foods:	Traditional Clothing:
Draw the Flag:	A Quote or Proverb:
A Historic Event:	A Famous Landmark:

Things to Know
when Traveling to
PARIS

_____

_____

_____

_____

_____

_____

_____

_____

_____

_____

_____

What to See

Write about a Historic Event
PARIS

_____

_____

_____

_____

_____

_____

_____

_____

_____

_____

_____

_____

What to Do

Find a Recipe From
PARIS

TITLE:

_____

Ingredients:

_____   _____

_____   _____

_____   _____

_____

Instructions:

_____

_____

_____

_____

Step by Step Food Prep:

1	2
3	4
5	6

All About Style

PARIS

Fashion in the City

_____

_____

_____

MODERN STYLES

Draw Traditional Costumes:

PRAGUE

CZECH REPUBLIC

All About

PRAGUE

Look in a Book
Look on Google Earth
Watch A Documentary

RESEARCH REFERENCES:

_____

_____

_____

NOTES:

_____

_____

_____

_____

Write or Draw

Popular Foods:	Traditional Clothing:

Draw the Flag:	A Quote or Proverb:

A Historic Event:	A Famous Landmark:

Things to Know when Traveling to PRAGUE

What to See

Write about a Historic Event
PRAGUE

_____

_____

_____

_____

_____

_____

_____

_____

_____

_____

_____

What to Do

Find a Recipe From
PRAGUE

TITLE:

_____

Ingredients:

_____   _____

_____   _____

_____   _____

_____

Instructions:

_____

_____

_____

_____

_____

Step by Step Food Prep:

1	2
3	4
5	6

All About Style

PRAGUE

Fashion in the City

_____

_____

_____

_____

MODERN STYLES

Draw Traditional Costumes:

Insert Image

RIO DE JANEIRO

BRAZIL

All About

RIO DE JANEIRO

Look in a Book
Look on Google Earth
Watch A Documentary

RESEARCH REFERENCES:

_____

_____

_____

NOTES:

_____

_____

_____

_____

Write or Draw

Popular Foods:	Traditional Clothing:

Draw the Flag:	A Quote or Proverb:

A Historic Event:	A Famous Landmark:

Things to Know
when Traveling to
RIO DE JANEIRO

_____

_____

_____

_____

_____

_____

_____

_____

_____

_____

_____

What to See

Write about a Historic Event
RIO DE JANEIRO

_____

_____

_____

_____

_____

_____

_____

_____

_____

_____

_____

_____

_____

What to Do

Find a Recipe From
RIO DE JANEIRO

TITLE:

_____

Ingredients:

_____   _____

_____   _____

_____   _____

_____

Instructions:

_____

_____

_____

_____

_____

Step by Step Food Prep:

1	2
3	4
5	6

RIO DE JANEIRO

Fashion in the City

_____

_____

_____

_____

MODERN STYLES

Draw Traditional Costumes:

Insert Image

ROME

ITALY

All About

ROME

Look in a Book
Look on Google Earth
Watch A Documentary

RESEARCH REFERENCES:

_____

_____

_____

NOTES:

_____

_____

_____

_____

_____

Write or Draw

Popular Foods:	Traditional Clothing:
Draw the Flag:	**A Quote or Proverb:**
A Historic Event:	**A Famous Landmark:**

Things to Know
when Traveling to
ROME

_____

_____

_____

_____

_____

_____

_____

_____

_____

_____

_____

What to See

Write about a Historic Event

ROME

_____

_____

_____

_____

_____

_____

_____

_____

_____

_____

_____

_____

What to Do

Find a Recipe From

ROME

TITLE:

_____

Ingredients:

_____   _____

_____   _____

_____   _____

_____

Instructions:

_____

_____

_____

_____

_____

Step by Step Food Prep:

1	2
3	4
5	6

All About Style

ROME

Fashion in the City

_____

_____

_____

_____

MODERN STYLES

Draw Traditional Costumes:

ST. PETERSBURG

SAINT PETERSBURG

RUSSIA

All About
SAINT PETERSBURG

Look in a Book
Look on Google Earth
Watch A Documentary

RESEARCH REFERENCES:

_____

_____

_____

NOTES:

_____

_____

_____

_____

_____

Write or Draw

Popular Foods:	Traditional Clothing:
Draw the Flag:	A Quote or Proverb:
A Historic Event:	A Famous Landmark:

Things to Know
when Traveling to
SAINT PETERSBURG

_____

_____

_____

_____

_____

_____

_____

_____

_____

_____

_____

_____

What to See

Write about a Historic Event

SAINT PETERSBURG

_____

_____

_____

_____

_____

_____

_____

_____

_____

_____

_____

_____

What to Do

Find a Recipe From
SAINT PETERSBURG

TITLE:

_____

Ingredients:

_____   _____

_____   _____

_____   _____

_____

Instructions:

_____

_____

_____

_____

_____

Step by Step Food Prep:

1	2
3	4
5	6

All About Style

SAINT PETERSBURG

Fashion in the City

_____

_____

_____

MODERN STYLES

Draw Traditional Costumes:

SAN FRANCISCO

SAN FRANCISCO

UNITED STATES
OF AMERICA

All About
SAN FRANCISCO

Look in a Book
Look on Google Earth
Watch A Documentary

RESEARCH REFERENCES:

_____

_____

_____

NOTES:

_____

_____

_____

_____

Write or Draw

Popular Foods:	Traditional Clothing:
Draw the Flag:	A Quote or Proverb:
A Historic Event:	A Famous Landmark:

Things to Know when Traveling to SAN FRANCISCO

_____

_____

_____

_____

_____

_____

_____

_____

_____

_____

_____

What to See

Write about a Historic Event

SAN FRANCISCO

_____

_____

_____

_____

_____

_____

_____

_____

_____

_____

_____

_____

What to Do

Find a Recipe From
SAN FRANCISCO

TITLE:

_____

Ingredients:

_____   _____

_____   _____

_____   _____

_____

Instructions:

_____

_____

_____

_____

_____

Step by Step Food Prep:

1	2
3	4
5	6

All About Style

SAN FRANCISCO

Fashion in the City

_____

_____

_____

_____

MODERN STYLES

Draw Traditional Costumes:

SEATTLE

UNITED STATES
OF AMERICA

All About
SEATTLE

Look in a Book
Look on Google Earth
Watch A Documentary

RESEARCH REFERENCES:

_____

_____

_____

NOTES:

_____

_____

_____

_____

_____

Write or Draw

Popular Foods:	Traditional Clothing:

Draw the Flag:	A Quote or Proverb:

A Historic Event:	A Famous Landmark:

Things to Know when Traveling to SEATTLE

_____

_____

_____

_____

_____

_____

_____

_____

_____

_____

_____

What to See

Write about a Historic Event

SEATTLE

_____

_____

_____

_____

_____

_____

_____

_____

_____

_____

_____

_____

What to Do

Find a Recipe From
SEATTLE

TITLE:

_____

Ingredients:

_____ _____

_____ _____

_____ _____

_____

Instructions:

_____

_____

_____

_____

_____

Step by Step Food Prep:

1	2
3	4
5	6

All About Style

SEATTLE

Fashion in the City

_____

_____

_____

_____

MODERN STYLES

Draw Traditional Costumes:

SHANGHAI

CHINA

All About

SHANGHAI

Look in a Book
Look on Google Earth
Watch A Documentary

RESEARCH REFERENCES:

_____

_____

_____

NOTES:

_____

_____

_____

_____

Write or Draw

Popular Foods:	Traditional Clothing:
Draw the Flag:	A Quote or Proverb:
A Historic Event:	A Famous Landmark:

Things to Know when Traveling to SHANGHAI

_____

_____

_____

_____

_____

_____

_____

_____

_____

_____

_____

What to See

Write about a Historic Event
SHANGHAI

_____

_____

_____

_____

_____

_____

_____

_____

_____

_____

_____

_____

What to Do

Find a Recipe From
SHANGHAI

TITLE:

_____

Ingredients:

_____   _____

_____   _____

_____   _____

_____

Instructions:

_____

_____

_____

_____

_____

Step by Step Food Prep:

1	2
3	4
5	6

All About Style

SHANGHAI

Fashion in the City

_____

_____

_____

_____

MODERN STYLES

Draw Traditional Costumes:

Singapore

SINGAPORE

SINGAPORE

All About
SINGAPORE

Look in a Book
Look on Google Earth
Watch A Documentary

RESEARCH REFERENCES:

_____

_____

_____

NOTES:

_____

_____

_____

_____

Write or Draw

Popular Foods:	Traditional Clothing:
Draw the Flag:	A Quote or Proverb:
A Historic Event:	A Famous Landmark:

Things to Know
when Traveling to
SINGAPORE

_____

_____

_____

_____

_____

_____

_____

_____

_____

_____

_____

_____

What to See

Write about a Historic Event
SINGAPORE

_____

_____

_____

_____

_____

_____

_____

_____

_____

_____

_____

_____

What to Do

Find a Recipe From
SINGAPORE

TITLE:

_____

Ingredients:

_____   _____

_____   _____

_____   _____

_____

Instructions:

_____

_____

_____

_____

_____

Step by Step Food Prep:

1	2
3	4
5	6

All About Style

SINGAPORE

Fashion in the City

_____

_____

_____

_____

MODERN STYLES

Draw Traditional Costumes:

STOCKHOLM

SWEDEN

All About
STOCKHOLM

Look in a Book
Look on Google Earth
Watch A Documentary

RESEARCH REFERENCES:

_____

_____

_____

NOTES:

_____

_____

_____

_____

_____

Write or Draw

Popular Foods:	Traditional Clothing:
Draw the Flag:	A Quote or Proverb:
A Historic Event:	A Famous Landmark:

Things to Know
when Traveling to
STOCKHOLM

_____

_____

_____

_____

_____

_____

_____

_____

_____

_____

_____

What to See

Write about a Historic Event
STOCKHOLM

What to Do

Find a Recipe From
STOCKHOLM

TITLE:

_____

Ingredients:

_____   _____

_____   _____

_____   _____

_____

Instructions:

_____

_____

_____

_____

Step by Step Food Prep:

1	2
3	4
5	6

All About Style

STOCKHOLM

Fashion in the City

_____

_____

_____

_____

MODERN STYLES

Draw Traditional Costumes:

SYDNEY

AUSTRALIA

All About
SYDNEY

Look in a Book
Look on Google Earth
Watch A Documentary

RESEARCH REFERENCES:

_____

_____

_____

NOTES:

_____

_____

_____

_____

Write or Draw

Popular Foods:	Traditional Clothing:

Draw the Flag:	A Quote or Proverb:

A Historic Event:	A Famous Landmark:

Things to Know
when Traveling to
SYDNEY

_____

_____

_____

_____

_____

_____

_____

_____

_____

_____

_____

What to See

Write about a Historic Event
SYDNEY

_____

_____

_____

_____

_____

_____

_____

_____

_____

_____

_____

_____

What to Do

Find a Recipe From
SYDNEY

TITLE:

_____

Ingredients:

_____   _____

_____   _____

_____   _____

_____

Instructions:

_____

_____

_____

_____

_____

Step by Step Food Prep:

1	2
3	4
5	6

All About Style

SYDNEY

Fashion in the City

_____

_____

_____

_____

MODERN STYLES

Draw Traditional Costumes:

TOKYO

JAPAN

All About
TOKYO

Look in a Book
Look on Google Earth
Watch A Documentary

RESEARCH REFERENCES:

_____

_____

_____

NOTES:

_____

_____

_____

_____

Write or Draw

Popular Foods:	Traditional Clothing:
Draw the Flag:	A Quote or Proverb:
A Historic Event:	A Famous Landmark:

Things to Know when Traveling to
TOKYO

_____

_____

_____

_____

_____

_____

_____

_____

_____

_____

_____

What to See

Write about a Historic Event
TOKYO

_____

_____

_____

_____

_____

_____

_____

_____

_____

_____

_____

What to Do

Find a Recipe From
TOKYO

TITLE:

_____

Ingredients:

_____   _____

_____   _____

_____   _____

_____

Instructions:

_____

_____

_____

_____

_____

Step by Step Food Prep:

1	2
3	4
5	6

All About Style

TOKYO

Fashion in the City

_____

_____

_____

_____

MODERN STYLES

Draw Traditional Costumes:

VANCOUVER

CANADA

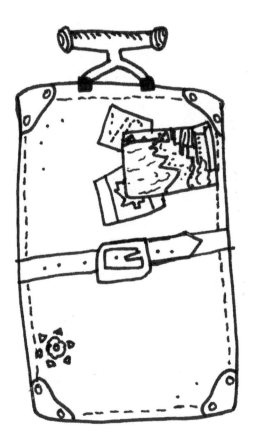

All About

VANCOUVER

Look in a Book
Look on Google Earth
Watch A Documentary

RESEARCH REFERENCES:

_____

_____

_____

NOTES:

_____

_____

_____

_____

Write or Draw

Popular Foods:	Traditional Clothing:
Draw the Flag:	A Quote or Proverb:
A Historic Event:	A Famous Landmark:

Things to Know when Traveling to

VANCOUVER

_____

_____

_____

_____

_____

_____

_____

_____

_____

_____

_____

What to See

Write about a Historic Event

VANCOUVER

_____

_____

_____

_____

_____

_____

_____

_____

_____

_____

_____

What to Do

Find a Recipe From
VANCOUVER

TITLE:

_____

Ingredients:

_____   _____

_____   _____

_____   _____

_____   _____

Instructions:

_____

_____

_____

_____

_____

Step by Step Food Prep:

1	2
3	4
5	6

All About Style

VANCOUVER

Fashion in the City

_____

_____

_____

_____

MODERN STYLES

Draw Traditional Costumes:

VENEZIA
GRAND CANAL

VENICE

ITALY

All About
VENICE

Look in a Book
Look on Google Earth
Watch A Documentary

RESEARCH REFERENCES:

_____

_____

_____

NOTES:

_____

_____

_____

_____

_____

Write or Draw

Popular Foods:	Traditional Clothing:
Draw the Flag:	A Quote or Proverb:
A Historic Event:	A Famous Landmark:

Things to Know
when Traveling to
VENICE

_____

_____

_____

_____

_____

_____

_____

_____

_____

_____

_____

What to See

Write about a Historic Event
VENICE

_____

_____

_____

_____

_____

_____

_____

_____

_____

_____

_____

_____

What to Do

Find a Recipe From
VENICE

TITLE:

_____

Ingredients:

_____   _____

_____   _____

_____   _____

_____   _____

Instructions:

_____

_____

_____

_____

Step by Step Food Prep:

1	2
3	4
5	6

All About Style

VENICE

Fashion in the City

_____

_____

_____

_____

MODERN STYLES

Draw Traditional Costumes:

WASHINGTON D.C.

UNITED STATES
OF AMERICA

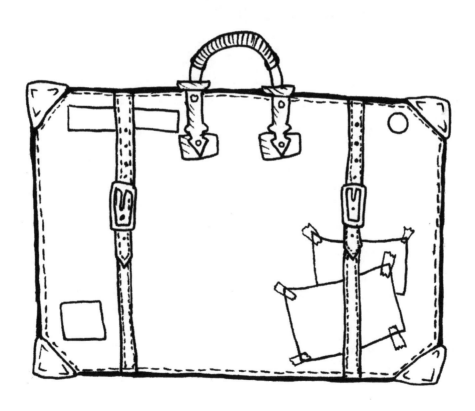

All About
WASHINGTON D.C.

Look in a Book
Look on Google Earth
Watch A Documentary

RESEARCH REFERENCES:

_____

_____

_____

NOTES:

_____

_____

_____

_____

_____

Write or Draw

Popular Foods:	Traditional Clothing:
Draw the Flag:	A Quote or Proverb:
A Historic Event:	A Famous Landmark:

Things to Know
when Traveling to
WASHINGTON D.C.

_____

_____

_____

_____

_____

_____

_____

_____

_____

_____

_____

What to See

Write about a Historic Event
WASHINGTON D.C.

_____

_____

_____

_____

_____

_____

_____

_____

_____

_____

_____

_____

_____

What to Do

Find a Recipe From
WASHINGTON D.C.

TITLE:

_____

Ingredients:

_____ _____

_____ _____

_____ _____

_____ _____

Instructions:

_____

_____

_____

_____

_____

Step by Step Food Prep:

1	2
3	4
5	6

All About Style

WASHINGTON D.C.

Fashion in the City

_____

_____

_____

_____

MODERN STYLES

Draw Traditional Costumes:

Zürich. Switzerland.

ZURICH

SWITZERLAND

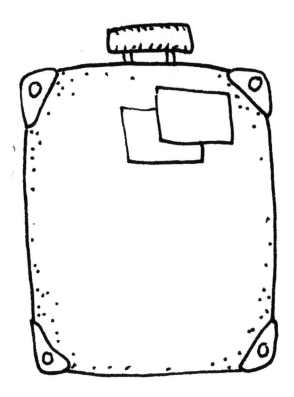

All About
ZURICH

Look in a Book
Look on Google Earth
Watch A Documentary

RESEARCH REFERENCES:

_____

_____

_____

NOTES:

_____

_____

_____

_____

_____

Write or Draw

Popular Foods:	Traditional Clothing:
Draw the Flag:	**A Quote or Proverb:**
A Historic Event:	**A Famous Landmark:**

Things to Know when Traveling to
ZURICH

_____

_____

_____

_____

_____

_____

_____

_____

_____

_____

_____

What to See

Write about a Historic Event
ZURICH

_____

_____

_____

_____

_____

_____

_____

_____

_____

_____

_____

_____

What to Do

Find a Recipe From
ZURICH

TITLE:

_____

Ingredients:

_____   _____

_____   _____

_____   _____

_____

Instructions:

_____

_____

_____

_____

_____

Step by Step Food Prep:

1	2
3	4
5	6

All About Style

ZURICH

Fashion in the City

_____

_____

_____

_____

MODERN STYLES

Draw Traditional Costumes:

Draw the Skyline

Draw the Skyline

Choose Your Own City:

_____

_____

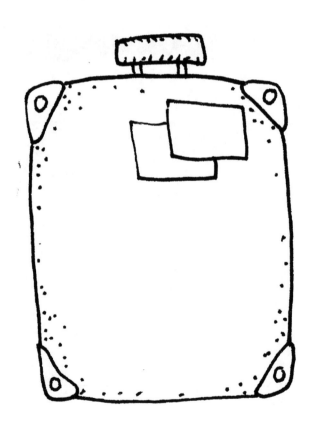

All About

_____

Look in a Book
Look on Google Earth
Watch A Documentary

RESEARCH REFERENCES:

_____

_____

_____

NOTES:

_____

_____

_____

_____

Write or Draw

Popular Foods:	Traditional Clothing:
Draw the Flag:	**A Quote or Proverb:**
A Historic Event:	**A Famous Landmark:**

Things to Know when Traveling to

_____

_____

_____

_____

_____

_____

_____

_____

_____

_____

_____

_____

What to See

Write about a Historic Event

_____

_____

_____

_____

_____

_____

_____

_____

_____

_____

_____

_____

_____

_____

What to Do

Find a Recipe From

_____

TITLE:

_____

Ingredients:

_____ _____

_____ _____

_____ _____

_____

Instructions:

_____

_____

_____

_____

Step by Step Food Prep:

1	2
3	4
5	6

All About Style

Fashion in the City

_____

_____

_____

_____

MODERN STYLES

Draw Traditional Costumes:

Draw the Skyline

Choose Your Own City:

_____

_____

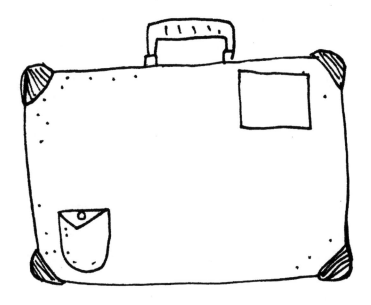

All About

_____

Look in a Book
Look on Google Earth
Watch A Documentary

RESEARCH REFERENCES:

_____

_____

_____

NOTES:

_____

_____

_____

_____

_____

Write or Draw

Popular Foods:	Traditional Clothing:
Draw the Flag:	A Quote or Proverb:
A Historic Event:	A Famous Landmark:

Things to Know
when Traveling to

_____

What to See

Write about a Historic Event

_____

_____

_____

_____

_____

_____

_____

_____

_____

_____

_____

_____

_____

What to Do

Find a Recipe From

_____

TITLE:

_____

Ingredients:

_____   _____

_____   _____

_____   _____

_____

Instructions:

_____

_____

_____

_____

_____

Step by Step Food Prep:

1	2
3	4
5	6

All About Style

Fashion in the City

MODERN STYLES

Draw Traditional Costumes:

Insert Image

Choose Your Own City:

_____

_____

All About

_____

Look in a Book
Look on Google Earth
Watch A Documentary

RESEARCH REFERENCES:

_____

_____

_____

NOTES:

_____

_____

_____

_____

_____

Write or Draw

Popular Foods:	Traditional Clothing:
Draw the Flag:	**A Quote or Proverb:**
A Historic Event:	**A Famous Landmark:**

Things to Know
when Traveling to

What to See

Write about a Historic Event

_____

_____

_____

_____

_____

_____

_____

_____

_____

_____

_____

_____

_____

What to Do

Find a Recipe From

_____

TITLE:

_____

Ingredients:

_____   _____

_____   _____

_____   _____

_____

Instructions:

_____

_____

_____

_____

_____

Step by Step Food Prep:

1	2
3	4
5	6

All About Style

_____

Fashion in the City

_____

_____

_____

_____

MODERN STYLES

Draw Traditional Costumes:

Travel Dreams

Brown Family Travels

This book was created by
Anna Brown, age 15.

The following pages are collages of
photos from Anna Brown's adventures!
Anna has been traveling with her
homeschooling family of twelve in
Europe since 2012.

We call it "Rome-Schooling"
With Josh & Sarah Brown
Isaac, Anna, Estera, Rachel, Naomi,
Susie, Laura, Joseph, Ember & Leah.

One Year in Italy

Five Months in Croatia

One Year in Ukraine

One Month in Austria

Four Days in France

Two Weeks in Germany

Two Weeks in England

Two Months in Portugal

Three Weeks in Hungary

Do It Yourself
HOMESCHOOL
JOURNALS

Copyright Information

Do It YOURSELF Homeschool Journal, and electronic printable downloads are for Home and Family use only. You may make copies of these materials for only the children in your household.

All other uses of this material must be permitted in writing by the Thinking Tree LLC. It is a violation of copyright law to distribute the electronic files or make copies for your friends, associates or students without our permission.

For information on using these materials for businesses, co-ops, summer camps, day camps, daycare, afterschool program, churches, or schools please contact us for licensing.

Contact Us:

The Thinking Tree LLC

617 N. Swope St. Greenfield, IN 46140. United States

317.622.8852 PHONE (Dial +1 outside of the USA) 267.712.7889 FAX

www.DyslexiaGames.com

jbrown@DyslexiaGames.com

THE Thinking TREE

PUBLISHING COMPANY

Sarah Janisse Brown

Made in the USA
San Bernardino, CA
24 May 2016